C'mon, Sell your House! It's Fun in a Flu Season Sort of Way!

A lighthearted look at maintaining perspective while selling your home

By: Doug Wilcoxon

C'mon, Sell your House! It's fun in a flu season sort of way!

Dedication

For my wife Wendy, you make every journey worthwhile. There is no other path I can imagine.

To my good friend Chet, thanks for taking a chance and hiring a guy off the street, for planting the seeds of ideation along the way, and becoming a friend who makes me a better person. Inspiration and all its synonyms apply to you.

For my cousin Steve Bonifield, who has inspired me with humor and intelligence since the days on the farm . . . and maybe before that, but we were pretty young so it's hard to recall. Your faith in me gives me faith in myself.

On an old typewriter my Grandma Wilcoxon would always pound out some quotes to prepare us for the days ahead. This was one of my favorites.

"Finish each day and be done with it. You have done what you could. Some blunders and absurdities no doubt crept in; forget them as soon as you can. Tomorrow is a new day. You shall begin it serenely and with too high a spirit to be encumbered with your old nonsense."

— Ralph Waldo Emerson

Table of Contents

Foreword

KNOW SOMEONE SELLING THEIR HOUSE?

READ THIS BOOK!

Chet Skwarcan, Engineer & Property Manager

I have known Doug Wilcoxon for 10 years. We have discussed the joys of property ownership, management and maintenance. I have been in his home several times and it's actually a lot like your home. It's well maintained, nicely decorated, and contains years of fond memories. Doug can tell you the story of each spot and every smell. Fortunately, when he decided to sell his home, the spots and smells, at the realtor's suggestion, were the first to go.

In these pages, Doug shares the personal, sometimes emotional, experience of selling his home. He shares insights, surprises, and a perspective that will help prepare you and, when necessary, calm you down. You will discover that selling your home does not always go the way you envisioned it. In fact, it never goes the way you envision it (so stop envisioning it!).

In this lighthearted read, Doug's technical background provides unusual objectivity to what can be an overly–emotional experience. His perspective appeals to the handyman as well as the housewife. You will find helpful tips on preparing to sell your home as well as coping with the unexpected.

Because Doug received a career offer he could not turn down, the timing of selling his home was somewhat unexpected. So, although he and his wife had made many improvements over the years and always did things right, there were still a few things to get in order. Keep in mind, Doug is not only a long–time property owner/manager, he is also an engineer. So, when he repaired something, he felt compelled to disassemble it, redesign it and save the leftover parts to build a dog polisher (and he doesn't even own a dog). This not only fulfilled his internal need to create and improve upon established design theory, but also meant an opportunity for him to buy more tools. His skill was tested to the limits when the house–selling process began.

Doug documents the highs and lows of selling a house to prepare you for the unexpected. You will see house selling through the eyes of the realtor, the potential buyer and, most importantly, the inspector. Some of the inspection reports will make you wonder if it is even legal to sell your house, especially when you consider the roof, the porch, the deck and radon issues. Don't get me wrong, Doug's house is in as good shape as any house I've been in (I've been in four homes to–date), but in the buyer's mind, it was impending doom. I'm exaggerating, but when someone criticizes your most expensive possession and the expression of your taste, it can hurt. Doug records this experience and his emotions along with tips on how to prepare and how to think objectively about the stages of selling your house.

I believe everything happens for a reason. Although Doug's experience may have been unique, I doubt it. The lessons he learned will encourage you and guide you toward a less stressful and more enjoyable home–selling experience. He encountered every nuance and issue known to modern–day home sellers and came through unscathed, well, maybe slightly scathed.

This is a must read for the first–time home seller, with great reminders for the rest of us. The real estate market is not what it used to be. If you, or someone you know, is thinking of selling your house, this book is for you.

Whether you are selling your first home or your fifth, you will enjoy learning from Doug's experience and benefit from increased emotional stability as the offers, counter offers and the inspection reports roll in. If you are not selling your house, you will laugh — and maybe cry — as you read Doug's humorous account of what one man learned and is willing to share with the rest of us.

Chet Skwarcan, Engineer & Property Manager

Preface

Why write this book? Initially it was to get the home selling experience off my chest, out of my mind and hope I live long enough to look back and laugh about it. Right now . . . there is not even a hint of a chuckle. It's about as much fun as chewing aluminum foil. As I write, we are in the midst of Buyer #3 (spoiler alert: Buyer #1 and Buyer #2 backed out). Inspection #3 is tomorrow, and we are wondering what will come up next . . .we can hardly wait since inspections are such an enjoyable experience. Will it be a happy ending? Can I write the last chapter and get on with my life and think of something other than . . . what the home inspector will think of next. Or will another chapter take shape . . . "Buyer #4 – A New Hope" . . . There seems to be a familiar ring to it.

We have bought and sold homes before. Quite a few really, but this time the experience is somehow different and I'm not sure why. Is it because banks are cracking down on inspectors so that they comment on each and every popped drywall nail? And where in the world do you even buy a popped drywall nail? Are buyers still holding on to the glory days of home buying after 2008 when homeowners were underwater and trying to minimize their losses? I'm not sure what drives the weirdness, but it makes one think in the abstract. Emotions can get out of control if you are not careful.

The story that follows is just this one seller's tongue in cheek perspective of his pilgrimage to sell the home him and his wife love, to someone he never sees, someone who lurks in the shadows and corresponds only through the impersonal black and white New Times Roman font of the Buyers Response Form (BRF).

Is it typical? The forms? The font? Probably so . . . the rest . . . I hope not, but maybe this story of our journey can help you maintain a detached perspective when you decide to experience the happy misery of selling your home. When you feel potential buyers are attacking your personal taste and inspectors make it seem as if the place is a derelict property maintained by a derelict owner — you can take a step back, take a deep breath and know you are not alone. Many have walked this well–worn path before you. Don't get caught up in the emotional minutiae that has no bearing on your wellbeing in the long run.

There are two sides to every story . . .well that's not quite true . . . when I was renting apartments to prospective tenants there were seven sides to every story. This story has only one side. My side . . . the seller's side . . . let's get on with it.

Doug Wilcoxon, Danville, IN 2015

Introduction

Selling your home is an emotional experience. This is your house, you have put down roots, given your blood, sweat and tears to make it a home, hosted a yearly family Thanksgiving and Christmas, watched nervously as your 16–year–old leaves the driveway for the first time on her own, squealing the tires to get anywhere but there (home), hosted birthdays and graduations, and shown the new "digs" proudly to your parents and grandparents. Every room has meaning. The carpet, the fixtures; every paint color carefully selected based on your tastes (at the time). This home is a part of you. That's great for you, the seller, but the buyer does not care.

The buyer views the house through a different lens. One lens is that of personal preference. They see a house with colors they don't like, landscaping they don't want to deal with, carpet a bit too crazy for their taste (who doesn't like carpet on the walls?), the 3 am disco club next door, a yard with weedy grass, a faded deck and no emotional attachment to the house in any sense. Another lens in the buyer's arsenal is that of the microscopic lens. If enough interest exists following the first viewing, the buyer will return with the aid of their paid inspector to destroy any of the remaining interest the buyer may have. "No little issue goes unpunished" is what I believe to be the creed of the home inspector.

Your memories are not going to sell the house. Buyers don't care about your memories, well they may care, but they will not pay you for them . . . if they do, you must be one special home seller, a reality TV celebrity or some internet freak or both. Buyers are looking to buy a house for themselves. It will sell based on their wishes and desires. Does the floor plan meet their needs? Is the house well maintained? Will the yard allow Spot to exercise and slip next door to poop in the neighbor's yard? Does it have a nine car garage and heliport? They are looking at the bottom line. How old is the property, the roof, the furnace. In their mind, this is a house, not yet a home, and it is a large investment.

Tip: Remember, to the buyer, this is a house ... not [yet] a home. Don't take others preferences and personal taste as an affront to your lifetime of decorating decisions. If you feel you have been insulted, talk about them in private, behind their back, or let the air out of their tires, but keep the sale moving forward.

Getting the Show on the Road

My wife is not a big fan of our long cold Indiana winters . . . so after our daughter's third year of employment at Disney World and her educating us to the benefits of living in sunny Orlando, Florida, we began to discuss a possible move from our home just outside of Indianapolis, to a more temperate locale. Of course the previous string of below freezing temperatures for a month and a half straight didn't hurt the cause. Our son, who is the last child out of the house, is finishing his senior year in college and we have become familiar with the empty nester lifestyle so we determined that with no one left to entertain at home (except my wife, who is not easily entertained by my knock–knock jokes) it was time to explore a potential move . . .

Fortunately at this juncture, the company I work for is laying down some strategery and expanding into Florida. It feels as though the time is right to discuss opportunities with one of our multi–talented executives. My thoughts are that maybe in one or two years a Florida position might become available and in that time we can prepare our house, take care of the maintenance that we deferred and get ourselves organized for a move to the Sunshine State!

Much to my surprise, the Florida expansion is a bit more aggressive than I realized (I must make it a point to attend the quarterly business meetings more often . . . at least quarterly). We have a productive discussion and come to general terms about the move, and he states "the sooner we can get to Florida the better". Thinking about the move and actually pulling the trigger to make the move are definitely two distinct feelings and when it's time to make it happen there tends to be a sense of unease and a heavy feeling in the pit of your stomach when you realize the enormity of the task at hand and the changes that are about to come forth. It is similar to the feeling you get when attempting the first kiss, but not as much fun, not as much excitement, and not as sweaty . . . so really it's not like that at all. Maybe it's more like standing in front of a large audience preparing to give a speech and thinking about how sweaty I got before that first kiss, except Grandma didn't mind, and Grandma wasn't sweaty (as I recall). In that case there also exists the sense of unease and a heavy feeling in the pit of the stomach.

TIP: Be careful what you ask for.

Timing Isn't Everything . . .
Or Is it?

The conversation with the multi–talented company executive regarding the potential move took place in October. "Sooner rather than later" was weighing down my synapses; well that and the binge watching on Netflix. Our kids are in their early 20's, but we knew they would want to come home and see the house one more time, say goodbye to old friends and make peace with the place where they grew up, and maybe help me re–roof the house (riiight). The teenage dreams of being anywhere but here have long faded (but then again neither one is here . . . hmmmmm). With November comes Thanksgiving and December brings Christmas, quickly followed by the New Year and at some point the cold winter sets in and people don't like to get out much in the frostbitten Indiana air.

These months are not only busy with families, holidays, cold weather and reruns, but can also be put to productive use planning for the sale of the home — all the cleaning and packing that go along with the initial preparations. The winter months are a good time to stay indoors. Indoors is where all the action begins when it's time to evaluate the retained mementos of our past 23 years; and as the holiday season arrives Thanksgiving and Christmas decorations can be displayed and then following the final holiday they can be sorted and donated, disposed, or kept and wrapped in newsprint and boxed for the move. Label your box.

Not all time has to be spent on holiday material goods, time can also be spent sorting through the collection of family heirlooms (some would say family junk) that has been collected for years, and some collected before I was born, but handed to me as the keeper of the family history (relatives are tricky). The winter months are a good time to sort through boxes and drawers that haven't been opened since the Great Depression, but it's also kind of fun to guess what is inside.

In my opinion it doesn't make sense to list the home anytime at the end of the year. There is just way too much going on with the holidays and the parties. It does seem a good time to spread the word of your upcoming move, maybe seek an active buyer. It might even give you thoughts about selling the home yourself (but a good night's sleep usually cures that thought).

Don't get too excited about selling the home yourself. Nobody wants to talk to the homeowner. For some strange reason the potential buyer doesn't want to have a face to face conversation regarding the home. They don't want to tell you everything they hate about your home or pitch the lowball offer out of fear that you will be insulted. The buyer would rather give the lowball offer through their realtor and give you their dislikes in writing where you can read them again and again.

And the dream of finding an active buyer . . . that's like finding a needle in a haystack, that's why realtors use the Multiple Listing Service (MLS). They want to spread that net as far as possible, get lots of looks. You may be thinking . . . I could tell all my friends and they could pass on the information . . . how far do you believe that will go . . . friends and coworkers aren't interested in selling your home. They don't have any skin in the game, they have their own lives to deal with, their own homes to maintain, and their own self to look at in the mirror. They aren't looking for a new place two blocks away to disrupt their lives for six months to a year. They probably already looked at your neighborhood when they moved to town and decided they didn't like it, but don't want to tell you because they don't want to watch you cry due to your fragile home seller state of mind. Side tip #1: If your friends seem really excited that you are moving, maybe you should take a closer look at that relationship. Side tip #2: If all your friends live in apartments, go ahead and spread the word . . . you never know unless you try.

Assuming you have the flexibility to wait, which we did, wait until the spring. Everything is blooming, birds are chirping, Bambi is running through the forest trying to escape the fire, humans are awakening from the winter slumber and thinking about the future, looking at a fresh start, making plans, getting some free time with a spring break, and beginning to forget about the large Christmas expenses accrued during November and December.

TIP: Sign up with a good Realtor early, accept and use to your advantage their experience and resources. They can help you determine items that may need repairs or improvements, offer advice with negotiations and get many more looks at your home than the For Sale by Owner sign in the front yard.

Realtor Cindy's Thoughts: *At one time the best time to sell a home was from the time school let out or June 1st to September 1st. Everyone wanted to move while school was out. Most buyers and sellers were families so that seemed to be the best time. Then people started getting job transfers, more single people started buying homes and in both of those instances they could be moving anytime during the year. Since I've been doing this for 39 years, I have seen the best time to sell change a lot. In 2014 from May through July everything that was halfway decent sold, then things came to a halt. The rest of the year came in waves, no showings one week, seven showings the next week. In November everything came to a screeching halt until . . . March, 2015. Then here we go again. Everything selling in days not weeks or months and that lasted through the end of May, then everything slowed down a lot.*

It's still pretty slow for the optimum months and who knows what the rest of the year will be. Generally, usually in the Midwest the spring is considered the best time to list your house with November through February being the worst. That said, I think almost anytime is a good time to sell, if it's in the Spring you will have more competition with more lookers than buyers where in December you will have very little competition but if someone's looking in December they are looking to buy, not just looking.

Unattended Home Repairs Get Their Day In Court

After the big decision is made to make the move and sell the home, we take a hard look at the state of repair or disrepair of our home. We always maintained the home and kept up with minor repairs during our 13 fabulous fun–filled years. Improvements were made, but the big ticket items such as the roof and heating and air units have never been replaced.

Roof

The roof is 18 years old. Over the years, leaks have dampened and discolored the ceiling in the living room and the master bathroom. After a storm, I would climb the roof, find the leak, remove the shingles and restore that small portion of the roof with new shingles. Usually it is a fairly obvious affair to locate the leak. In every instance the leak occurred at a roof vent or the boot of a vent pipe.

Repairs can be made to the roof to extend its useful life. The repairs are easy but the replacement shingles typically don't match and the roof will look old and worn because it has been beat up by the sun, wind and rain and it IS old and worn out. It could be a coincidence, but it seems that every home within spittin' distance of our place has had a new roof within the last three years. Potential buyers will notice the difference between your old roof and the shiny new ones.

TIP: Look at the neighbors' roofs and compare. You may not need to replace it, but it is a big bargaining chip for the buyer and it will most surely be pointed out by the buyers' [evil] home inspector.

A final note regarding shingles: "dimensional" shingles also known as architectural shingles (or laminated) are all the rage. The shingles do look nicer than a standard 3–tab and apparently are of a heavier construction providing a more durable shingle and longer life. I should sell shingles throwing down verbiage like that.

An analogy for your old roof. Picture if you will.... you are sitting at a traffic signal in your silverustish 1996 four cylinder Chevy S10. It runs well, not very fast, a dent on the driver's side over the front wheel and another on the passenger side in the bed panel. The driver's door mirror is missing, the temperature control knobs have broken off long ago, the cassette player doesn't work and a Mickey Mouse topper sitting proudly atop the antenna. Pulling up next to you at the traffic signal is a Carmine Red 2015 Porsche Cayenne. Guess which one is your roof?

Heating and Air Systems

Take care of heating and air units. Get yearly maintenance and change the filter. What else can you do . . . my wife likes the heat so we don't run the a/c much in the summer; obviously you don't want to extend the life of the unit through your own personal discomfort. I do, but only because I love my wife and care deeply about her comfort at the sacrifice of my own. I'm not bitter. :)

Our furnace and a/c operate well, but age is a factor that the seller has to consider. Older buyers tend to get chilled easily and that's why they wear sweaters. Sweaters were big in the 80's during the Cosby show, but sweater budgets can get expensive. That is why it's important to maintain your heating and air systems. In order to provide some peace of mind to the buyer you can offer a "home warranty" that covers the cost associated with basic heating and cooling units (a home warranty costs about $300–$400 FYI).

Furnace etiquette for the showing: keep the area around the furnace clear and clean. Make sure the condensate drain is draining to a proper location and not running across the basement floor or dropping into the crawl space or into a shoe box marked "crayons" (for example).

TIP: Maintain the furnace and a/c unit. It's easier as you go than all at once.

Realtor Cindy's Thoughts: *A home warranty is very important as far as I'm concerned. It gives a buyer peace of mind that if anything major happens during the first year they will not be out thousands of dollars for repairs. I would say 99% of all home buyers will expect a seller to provide them with a home warranty at closing. For the seller if they agree to provide a home warranty to the buyer, they will be covered for the life of the listing and you don't pay for the warranty until the closing. It also eliminates those pesky phone calls right after the closing when the buyers move in and the furnace isn't working. Just tell them to call the warranty company.*

<u>Outdoor Living – The Deck</u>

We built a detached patio in the back yard and created a great landscaped area. It is a very natural setup. Shaded and peaceful it provides a great place to relax, it's something Thoreau would find inviting . . . well maybe not, since he's dead and all. The attached deck however, is another story . . . it could have its own sequel, but I will condense it to a couple paragraphs . . . the Cliff Notes version. While we constructed a beautiful setting away from the house, the attached deck was falling into disrepair and tilting in a very noticeable fun–house sort of way.

I didn't touch the deck in 13 years, other than to walk on it . . . and to be honest, I have gained some weight, but that has absolutely nothing to do with the tilt. Although adjacent to the house, it is not actually "attached" to the house and has settled about six to eight inches. The foam insulating board covering the frame of the home is exposed. The two support posts adjacent to the house have been slowly settling into the basement backfill over the years. The settlement appears to have stopped, but it's very noticeable and the deck is in a sad state. Apparently the compaction of the soil after backfilling along the basement wall and proper post support for the deck was not a high priority for the home builder. Every buyer who has looked at our home has included the sagging deck as an issue either to fix or deduct from the asking price. So much for my idea to use it as a selling feature (Fun–House Deck! The only one in the neighborhood!).

TIP: Don't leave anything unattended for 13 years (That includes relationships too... I'm not speaking from experience or anything, I'm just sayin').

The patio area is a good place to sit and think. It's also a good place to sit and look at the back of the house, which is where the deck sits in all its settled glory. No longer desiring to look at the sinking deck, I turned my patio chair to face a different direction. This worked for a time, but realizing potential buyers may not think of that nifty fix we decided to repair and paint the deck to remove any possible objection before potential buyers could hammer it home in the inspection report. With some Yankee ingenuity we repaired the deck. It could now be crossed off the semi large big ticket items waiting to be repaired.

TIP: Don't leave the big ticket items for the buyer. When they are spending 100's of thousands they don't want to consider spending thousands more to repair "their new home". If you do leave big ticket items don't

plan on getting top dollar . . . unless you get lucky . . . and I heard sometimes that happens.

Front Entry

Speaking of basement backfill settling (what a great topic for cocktail parties or if you are in your 20's, Raves, but if you are in your 20's you're probably not a seller or reading this book . . . so never mind) . . . meanwhile . . . on the front side of the house, the entry leading to the front door had settled. This area is also within the limits of the basement backfill. It settled about four inches and hasn't moved in years. The green foam board is visible between the bottom trim of the siding and the top of the step. The step was like this when we moved in. We didn't consider it a factor, didn't even give it a second thought.

Buyers and their Realtors do give it a second thought. As a matter of fact, they give it a first thought. It is amazing how many comments are made about the entry settlement. It wasn't even on our radar when we made our to–do list of improvements and maintenance prior to the big sale. As the front entry reviews continue to roll in, I give it some serious thought.

Tip: Evaluate your entry. First impressions are important. Clean it up, make repairs as needed don't let the buyer start with a negative impression.

Of course it doesn't just stop with the basic settlement comment. One buyer's realtor accused us of hiding something because the step had settled. There must be a greater problem because the entry concrete appears to be a different color and texture of the sidewalk... so 'what are you hiding?' is the loaded question. Apparently people who sell homes are not trustworthy.

Every solution provided by the buyer's realtor is to tear it out and replace it. It seems that most of their solutions to any problem are costly (and maybe they are, but that is where they prefer to start). It pays to ask around, search the internet, and determine what options are available for the repairs to be made.

In the case of the front entry we found a better solution. Mudjacking: a common practice to raise concrete slabs and steps. Two or three small holes are drilled in areas where the settlement has occurred then a grout is injected into the hole. The grout begins to fill the void and raise the slab. There is a danger of cracking the slab if something is holding it in place, but the results are astounding and it is much faster, cleaner and neater than ripping it out and replacing.

TIP: Ask your friends, coworkers and neighbors how they have solved similar issues. They may be smarter than they look . . . just kidding, I have no idea what your neighbors look like. Research repairs on the internet. YouTube is a great resource for repairs. It has millions of videos and probably has one that speaks to your issue directly, by name.

Final Thoughts on improvements

Our kids are no longer at home and for the most part are self–sufficient, but we have been paying college expenses as we proceed down the road of college indebtedness. We made the decision to pay college expenses as we go and delay improvements until college is complete.

We hadn't given that theory too much thought before it was implemented, but the student loans are hard to stomach when you realize the debt your child is piling on as they enter their early twenties. We made the sacrifice to pay as much of the college expenses as we could. Of course that put a stop to a couple of the ongoing improvement projects.

In fact, we removed the carpet and the trim in the master bedroom and completely cleaned out the master bedroom closet. Initially we planned to put hardwood in the master bedroom and closet, but since we started the pay as you go program for college, the hardwood took a back seat and we lived on the plywood floor for a couple of years. After some time you get use to the semi rough surface and splinters in your feet. My wife spruced up the plywood by drawing smiley faces where the knots were in the plywood. It was a nice addition and a friendly face at the end of a long day.

SELLER TIP: Save money for your kid's college and plan the home improvements to accommodate the budget so it can be finished before your youngest celebrates his silver wedding anniversary.

Let's Get Real . . . My Thoughts on the Realtor

When I was young I tended to be a bit hard headed (cousin Steve still thinks the label applies), and maybe that is true for all youngsters... thinking I could do everything myself . . . I'm pretty resourceful, know my way around the internet, kind of smart, have a great Coney Dog recipe, and in the past I didn't think a realtor was important to the process. I would just hire an attorney to process the paperwork or try to sell it myself and worry about it later.

I don't believe that is the smart play any longer. Maybe back in the day you could get by on a wing and a prayer, but home buyers these days want every i dotted and t crossed. They will research and read everything on the internet related to the home buying process, whether it is a valid resource or not, and commit it to memory. It is because of this and the reasons stated throughout where I extoll the virtues of your realtor as you take this magical journey together.

With so many legal documents and issues relating to the sale of the home, ownership of the home and property (clear title), it is the smart move to have a person in your corner that understands the process, someone who deals with these issues day in and day out. Most closings are routine, but if something isn't routine, or if something is missing from the process, you will not be the one to notice. It will be your seasoned realtor who will notice something is different and bring it to your attention.

Some of you may be thinking . . . "But all they do is list it on the MLS, put a sign out front and sit back raking in 5, 6 or 7 percent. I can list it and save myself the money". Maybe you can do that, but for most of us this is our largest investment and the largest transaction we will make. It is a transaction in which we don't have much knowledge regarding the process or the applicable laws. Why take a chance with your greatest investment?

A Realtor from the National Associations of Realtors (NAR) is a good place to start. It is a real estate trade organization committed to the ethical practice of residential and commercial real estate for all aspects of the real estate business. The NAR supports their members and accordingly it is likely your realtor will be more knowledgeable, have access to more resources and if needed, have the ability to seek advice from the largest trade associations in the United States.

How did we select our realtor? For 13 years we lived in the same neighborhood and it may not have been every day, but more often than not when a sign went up around our neighborhood it was the same realtor with the same company, Cindy Martin, RE/MAX. I didn't know her at the time, but when I would ask about Cindy people would say she was a specialist at selling homes in our neighborhood. I would have to agree. Those for sale signs didn't stay up long. So when the time came she was the only person we called. We met and discussed our home and signed the papers all the same evening. There was no doubt in my mind that we were in good hands.

Proper pricing is always a concern. I had no idea how to set the home's initial asking price. During the initial meeting with Cindy she had already pulled the comps (comparables) of similar homes that sold recently within the neighborhood and explained each of the homes similarities and differences to our own. It was an enlightening experience as we were able to review and compare each home. Based on this information and her understanding of the local real estate market, she provided us with her estimate of the initial asking price. Prior to this meeting I had developed what I thought was an initial estimate for the value of the home. I had underestimated the value by almost 15%. I'm not saying that is going to happen in every case, maybe you are a better estimator than I am, but already our realtor has earned her commission and then some.

While we all have great taste, the unbiased eye of your realtor can provide you with some tips to improve the showing of your home. Maybe she will recommend moving the coffin out of the basement or repainting your black light room, cleaning up the stack of Playboy magazines you have collected since 1955. Some of those things might not appeal to the home buying public. Some may, but the odds are not in your favor. Our realtor has sold lots of homes, she knew what items required some touch up and what improvements could be made that would improve the showing of the home and therefore help speed along the sell. Let your Realtor give you the advice to help sell the home. It will be some work, but well worth it in the long run.

Obviously I believe it is beneficial to use the services of a professional who deals in the sale of residential properties day in and day out. With their knowledge of the market and understanding of the process, it will relieve a lot of stress and help minimize the risk that something was missed when processing the offers and at closing. We were happy with the assistance and guidance of our realtor throughout the process of selling our home. When a question needed to be asked or clarified we could make the phone call, issue resolved. I do believe that those best qualified are those who perform these services for a living. After all you don't want a plumber teaching you the Lambada.

Buyers Give Me Bad Dreams

We have lived in this home for 13 years and loved the floorplan from the beginning. It provided us with flexibility and we felt the possibilities were there for us to do some tweaking to the layout. We prefer a casual home with an open floor plan. We like it to be relaxing and inviting to family and guests. Nothing pretentious or too flashy.

Not everyone looks at possibilities. As a matter of fact, it seems that most buyers do not see possibilities, but only see what is presented. There is nothing imaginative about the mindset. The only thing visible lies at the end of the nose. It is very literal. It drives me crazy, but we already bought this house so it's not our fight, it's what we were looking for when it was our turn to be the buyers. I am certain buyers look at things quite differently than my wife or me. The question now is, what is the buyer looking for?

As far as I can tell, they want a home that fits their needs and their preferences. Most buyers are not skilled in the art of home construction, remodeling and repair. They want a home that matches most closely with their lifestyle that isn't going to require additional work. If they see the possibilities they know that any improvement for remodel is going to cost money. Why make the investment on a home that doesn't fit your needs? You as the seller want top dollar. The buyer wants the best house for the best price. Remember the competing interests of the buyer and seller when negotiations begin. It can help you think with a clear mind.

Tip: Don't make it personal when negotiating.

A final note. If you want to do some reading on behavioral economics search the term "endowment effect". It is the hypothesis that people ascribe more value to things merely because they own them. Think about that a minute and then go ahead and list it for top dollar because you own it and it's worth it.

When The Deal Is Going Smoothly . . . The Inspector May Rain On Your Parade

Over and over I repeat to myself "Inspectors are human, inspectors are human, inspectors are human". No matter how much it pains me to say it I must believe they have a family who loves them and waits for them to come home, where they return each night to do what humans do . . . maybe watch some TV, have some dinner, talk with the kids, burn ants with a magnifying glass, etc. Surely they don't go home and throw darts at a target labeled with random home deficiencies to gauge the home buyer's resistance to over the top verbiage. It seems for our home, the inspectors' goal is to describe the findings in the most horrific terms possible in order to make the potential buyer question your motives and integrity. Do these guys work for TMZ? Maybe I'm being punk'd.

I want to believe it is the family the inspector returns home to each night, but after two grueling inspections and two broken deals I am beginning to wonder. Maybe home inspectors consider it a badge of honor as to their effectiveness to the number of agreements that can be cast asunder. Unfortunately, 99% of home inspectors give the rest a bad name.

The ranting does make me feel better, but maybe I need to slow down, relax and think about this for a bit. I shouldn't be casting aspersions and making broad generalizations. This isn't some reality TV show. These are regular people working to make a living. Let me take a step back. I am just venting and you will probably want to vent too. I am sure inspectors are people of integrity trying to do a good job. I do inspections . . . not home inspections, but I understand that people who are getting inspected are nervous, and I also know that every inspector is different. Different inspectors focus on different things, but I would say most are trying to do a good job and everyone has a bad day from time to time. It's also true that some feel they must find something because nobody is perfect, which is true . . . just don't describe it as the worst condition since the black plague. A friend once suggested to leave some simple items for the inspector to find, that way they feel they are doing their job and don't have to look for random targets just to make a statement and "earn their fee". So, I put plaid pillows on our floral sofa and an extra refrigerator on the porch, but he didn't even notice.

Inspectors will do their job as they are required. Hopefully the buyer's agent will have the experience to understand the report and your buyer will have knowledge and understanding of the realities of maintaining a home and the severity of the items noted within the inspector's report. But if I were a gambling man I wouldn't make that bet.

After the inspection report is submitted, the buyer will come back with to–do items to be completed for the deal to move forward. Keep this in mind when negotiating a price for the home. That to–do list will cost money. If you can do it yourself and you are aware something needs to be fixed, I recommend fixing the problem prior to the inspection. If you don't, the typical request is accompanied by the phrase "to be completed by a qualified contractor". Which means even for an easy fix it's too late for you to do it and it will cost more $$$$.

TIP: The buyer picks the inspector, let them do their job and be realistic regarding the condition of your home.

Some Say The First Buyer Is The Best, Some Don't Say That . . . I'm One Of Those Who Don't Say That – Buyer #1

The home was on the market for a couple of weeks when the first offer was received from Buyer #1. We accepted the offer and all indications were positive with good feedback and what seemed a real interest in the qualities of the home. These were first time home buyers and they were very excited and loved the home. What could go wrong? Florida here we come.

The inspection report was well written and organized. Every issue or maintenance item noted was one that I was aware of except one. Cracks... this inspector noted cracks in the crawl space foundation. I knew the cracks were there because I have been looking at them every time I mow the grass. They have been in the foundation since I can remember; I never gave them a second thought. We have been here 13 years.

I mentioned earlier that I am an inspector. What I inspect are precast concrete plants. I have a fairly good understanding of concrete and I also know that concrete cracks. Every crack in the wall was from the corner of a crawlspace vents. Corners are high stress points that typically lead to cracking (are you snoring yet?). Measures can be taken to reduce the cracking during construction, but the builder didn't take the time to add additional steel to keep cracking to a minimum and new homeowners probably don't want to pay for the added steel. It's just the way of the world

The inspector noted to have the cracks inspected by a qualified foundation contractor. This is where I took exception to the person performing the inspections recommending the repairs. The contractor is going to complete the inspection and then perform the work based on his own recommendation. Call me old fashioned, but I consider this a bit of a conflict of interest. What license does this "qualified foundation contractor" hold to determine the structural integrity of the foundation.

I hired a structural engineer to evaluate the crawlspace foundation cracks. Where I work, we have structural engineers, but in the engineering field it is considered unethical to ask a coworker so I asked an architect friend to refer me to a structural engineer who evaluates foundations. That referral referred me to the structural engineer who does just that. I called him and scheduled an appointment. He arrived, completed the review of the crawlspace foundation and provided me a letter with his professional engineering seal confirming the structural integrity of the foundation.

All Good?

Not quite.

Apparently that wasn't satisfactory to the buyer or maybe the buyer's realtor. Who knows? You never get a chance to discuss it with them or meet them so you are pissing in the wind. The buyer requested that their foundation contractor look at the foundation. This is where you can't let it get personal. The buyer's realtor questioned my relationship with the structural engineer without asking how the engineer was selected. You know . . . since I'm an engineer and apparently all engineers know each other . . . logical?

We agreed to let the contractor look at the foundation to keep things moving. This is where it gets interesting (how many chapters and now it gets interesting). I know you are going to find it hard to believe, but the "qualified foundation contractor" goes into the crawl space with the buyer's boyfriend, crawls out a half hour later with a grim look on his face and tells me that foundation could or could not settle and cause damage to the home. The way this guy describes the situation, it sounds like the foundation could split in half and slide off into the street at any time. I know serious foundation cracks, you sir are no serious foundation crack (Thanks to Lloyd Bentsen for that quote reference). The house has stood for 18 years and doesn't exhibit the telltale signs of movement (such as damaged drywall).

Fortunately this contractor/inspector will be able to take care of this situation and it will only cost about $8000 to fix. I am not surprised and am not very amused. Now I wonder how often the realtor and foundation guy work this scam on other homeowners to make a little extra. What is their relationship? Homeowners who are a bit desperate to sell may have this work done. Is it time to question their integrity . . . NO. Keep moving forward.

I tell the contractor and the buyer's realtor that we will not be making those modifications. I ask the contractor to provide me with his findings, his estimate and his licenses so I can understand the issue he has found and what license he holds to make that determination. Interestingly, only the estimate was provided. The title of the "qualified foundation contractor" was Waterproofing and Foundation Repair Specialist.

We receive a mutual release. The deal is dead. Should we go after the earnest money? I believe we have a case, but don't want to be moving forward dealing with the negativity of a deal gone bad fighting over a $500 deposit which doesn't even amount to one–half of one percent of the asking price (in fact, it is not even ⅓ of ½ of 5%). Release . . .and it feels so gooood. (Thanks Peaches & Herb) The objective is to sell the house, not diddle over earnest money.

Tip: Understand who the ultimate authority is regarding the issue at hand. In this case a licensed structural engineer is granted that authority by the state through its licensing requirements. A contractor who makes evaluations of the structural integrity of your home is not. Also understand that, apparently, this may not matter.

Tip: The house isn't sold until the day of closing, after the signatures are on the contracts, and after you have left town and changed your names. In most cases the last two items may be skipped.

A final note: Apparently the buyer's realtor didn't understand the difference between a qualified contractor and licensed structural engineer. Not only did it kill the deal, but the buyer didn't get a good home (of course I am biased . . . I am the seller). If licensing isn't held in high regard to the buyer's realtor, then why is a license required to sell a home? Why not ask the "qualified foundation contractor" to sell your home or the Schwan salesman.... they do have very good cookies and they deliver to your door.

The Best Buyer Is The Last Buyer.... This Is Not The Best Buyer – Buyer #2

A month and a half has passed since our home was placed on the market. The home goes back on the market and Buyer #2 arrives shortly thereafter. This buyer starts with what I would consider a low ball offer. Not so low that you are offended and don't counter, but low enough to give it a whirl to see if the seller is biting. We drop a couple thou and toss it back over the fence. The buyer comes back with a better offer.

The offer is better and Buyer #2's agent states the offer is as high as they can go because of the work needing done to the exterior of the home. Our Realtor emails and asks to what work they are referring. Buyer #2's agent responds that the roof is 18 years old, the front entry is settling and the back deck is settling. We agree with the assessment and believe the buyers are savvy in this regard to point out the items requiring some upgrades. Because the buyers and their realtor assure us that they want the home for less but will take on the repairs mentioned we decide to accept their lower offered price and proceed. These aren't first time homebuyers so we assume we are working with buyers who are more knowledgeable about the process. We sign their counter offer and move forward awaiting the inspection.

The inspection is complete and Buyer #2 sends over the inspection response. In an uninteresting development, buyer #2's inspector identified the three items noted by the buyers in the counter which was used to set their maximum offer (it was expected). This inspector notes that the roof is exhibiting hail damage. The surprise portion of the inspection response from buyer #2 includes 1. A new roof. 2. Tear out the front entry and replace. 3. Raise the deck and attach to the house. So much for the buyer's initial statement in the bargain .. buyers can be tricky.

We state in our response that we will contact the insurance agent to evaluate the roof and ask for seven days to schedule. Buyer #2 responds that they no longer want the house and send over a mutual release. We ask for the earnest money since Buyer #2 backed out of the agreement.

As quickly as you can say "The earnest money goes to seller", Buyer #2 decides there is much more wrong with the house and begins to state issues and possible causes that were previously not a consideration during the negotiations. Not when they made the first offer and not after the home inspection. Apparently this buyer and agent begin to question our integrity and wonder what we are hiding. It has become apparent that a seller's integrity is suspect when the buyer backs out of an agreement, or the seller doesn't agree with the hack of a "qualified foundation specialist" and the buyer wants their money back. I'm learning this is all part of the fun.

In my humble opinion, earnest money doesn't mean diddly–squat. Especially earnest money in the low ball ranges. Sellers should require the buyer to pony up some real cash when they make an offer. In doing this, I believe it will make the buyer give the purchase the consideration it deserves before an agreement is signed. Since the day the house was on the market, the time spent negotiating with Buyer #1 and Buyer #2, the home has been tied up in purchase agreements and inspections longer than it has been available for sale.

We sign a mutual release and return the earnest money to the buyers. As before . . . the goal is to sell the home. I don't want to be dealing with Negative Nellies tossing accusations in order to get their earnest money. Let them go and out of your life. Say no to negativity, wait, no, I mean don't say yes to negativity, wait, never mind, just don't say anything.

Tip: Focus on the home sale, not on earnest money. Buyers will rationalize all day, all month, all year to get their money back. Just move on.

Realtor Cindy's Thoughts: *As far as the earnest money, ah, yes, the earnest money. At one time the normal amount of earnest money was 1% of the purchase price. Then agency came along where you had buyer agents, seller agents and limited agents (represent both parties). A buyer's agent wants their buyer to put the least amount of earnest money down in case there is a dispute and a seller's agent would like more earnest money down for the same reason. It seems like we've sort of settled in with $500 being the norm for purchase prices less than $150,000, $1,000 for $150,000 to $250,000 and on. This is one of my hot buttons. Earnest money is showing the seller that you are "earnest" about buying their home and are putting down money to prove that. They sign a contract, a binding agreement and, unless something comes up like a major defect that the seller will not correct, they should abide by the contract and we close and the buyer's earnest money is credited to them. I expect people to honor their word and the contract they signed and if they change their mind they forfeit their earnest money. As you know so well this is not the case. Buyers (and their agents in most cases) will try every trick in the book to not only get out of the contract but get their earnest money back. You are correct, the more money a buyer puts down as earnest money should make them think twice about just walking away from a signed contract. I think since it is currently a seller's market that we should ask for more earnest money but a lot of sellers don't want to counter back asking for more earnest money since it might mess up the home selling. I wish we could go back to the 1% but everything is negotiable so we can't make that a rule*

Soul Searching Between Buyer #2 and Buyer #3 (Queue Soft Music)

The big three items (roof, deck, entry) came up a few more times during some showings. We had been willing to negotiate these items but, based on the experience of the last couple of months, buyers believe you are lacking integrity, unethical or hiding something if a part of your home isn't perfect. Maybe those buyers should consider a building a home.

I was aware of the roof and deck, but had not given the front entry much thought. It had never been an issue with us. We just stepped a little higher to get into the front door (it worked the calf muscles, however I should mention here that we sold the calf several years ago when we put in new carpet). We decided to take care of the front entry before another buyer could see the house.

As we sat on the patio one afternoon relaxing after a day of yard work (we like yard work, some don't) it struck me how to raise the deck and attach it to the house (no, not mudjacking). I had a plan formulated and was able to complete the repairs in a day. The deck steps took another day and the cleaning and painting took a few more days. It was a simple fix once we thought about saving the deck.

The deck was always something I planned to redesign and build new, but after considering a total rebuild, we opted to repair the existing deck — kind of a phoenix rising from the ashes if you will. Maybe not quite that dramatic, more like a phoenix being pressure–washed and painted.

All that remains is the roof. Initially I assumed we would negotiate the roof age as part of the purchase price, but buyers don't want to negotiate the big ticket items. As fun as it sounds, no one wanted to play guess–the–age–of–the–roof. So, time for a new roof.

I have put on a few new roofs in the past, but my wife felt that I was younger and in better shape, which I was. I tossed around doing it myself, putting on a second layer and working on it in the evenings. Apparently nobody goes for that method anymore... so maybe I am getting older, not keeping current on roof etiquette. I still want to do it, but finding friends to volunteer to strip a roof and put on a new one is a difficult task. I have high expectations for my friends. It basically comes down to finding younger friends.

We decide to hire the work and have the new roof installed. With the new roof comes a warranty (buyers love warranties) and the warranty transfers to the buyer.

Why take care of the big three (roof, deck, entry)? I tired of thinking in terms of giveaways to the buyer. Now I know where I stand with regard to the asking price and there isn't much room for negotiation (at least in my mind). Of these three items that were repeatedly hammered by the inspectors (as expected) only the roof replacement was the costly option, but that was the tradeoff between paying the contractor to do the work or me doing the work, then keeling over from heat exhaustion, rolling down the roof, grasping for a gutter as I slide over the edge, ruining our raspberry bushes, lying on the ground wondering what I was doing, watching storm clouds assemble as rain begins to deluge the partially covered roof while I pick thorns from my hind quarters. We figured a contractor was a better option.

Third Time's A Charm – Buyer #3

Like George Washington, I cannot tell a lie (or was it Parson Weems?). Buyer #3's name sounds familiar to my wife and she is certain she knows the buyer (which she does) and Buyer #3 knows my wife. They knew each other through the school system. There is a trust between the buyers and sellers that didn't exist with the prior buyers. It begs the question: Is this type of trust possible between strangers as they work toward the completion of an agreement? Based on previous experience I would have to say no. It is not possible to develop this type of trust between strangers. This trust is developed through a shared experience.

So, the lesson here is that when Buyer #1 comes along, try to get to know them. Maybe go to a movie or out to dinner a few times. Explain to them that although you truly want to sell them your house, it just won't work unless you get to know each other. Show them some of the repairs you made and the humorous ways you fixed things. Try to get them laughing about all the new paint and carpeting because c'mon, pet stains are funny.

When discussing the sale of the home with friends we heard a number of times that the third time's a charm. I wanted to believe it, I was hopeful, but I was hopeful on all the others. Now I'm just pragmatic and that sounds really boring. Maybe pragmatic is the new normal. It crossed my mind that after two previous inspections there wasn't much left for the home inspector to comment on since all the repairs previously noted have been completed. Hopefully they didn't find Al Capone's vault in the crawl space. I'm not sure what I could do with those issues. (If you're under 50 you probably won't understand the Capone remark, but you're young so really it doesn't matter and it's really not relevant for your age bracket or this story, but that joke was just sitting there like low hanging fruit and I had to pick it from the tree of not so funny jokes. If you really want to know . . . Google it. You will also determine the joke was not that good.)

Buyer #3 arrived before the trifecta of major improvements were completed, but was informed of the improvements prior to the showing. The buyer made an offer and we accepted. Actually there were two offers that day so things were looking up. We accepted one and rejected the other.

We considered accepting both offers because we really could have used the money. The realtor mentioned something about "jail time" and based on my friend's experience, that is not something we wanted to risk. We also thought about rejecting both offers, just to save time, but again our realtor talked us out of it. Apparently statistics imply that houses sell more quickly when an offer has been accepted. So, like I said, we accepted one and rejected the other.

There was some back and forth, but it related only to clarifying items in the contract. The purchase price stood as it was initially made and the inspection was completed. At this point with the other buyers, it was the inspection that busted each agreement, so this time I am patiently waiting for the inspection guillotine to fall and drop some part of the agreement into the basket.

The inspection is received and as is typical with the other inspections there are items and comments that make me wince when I read them (maybe I'm getting too sensitive about this and need to listen to my own advice, maybe I simply wince too easily). The buyer's inspection response is requesting reasonable repairs plus now there is a drainage question. Drainage is a funny thing . . . water goes to the lowest point – this season we had record rains and the drainage swale in the back yard is wet because of that and the constant feed from the sump pump. The buyer wants to get clarification regarding the standing water (fair question). Which makes me think . . . isn't that odd terminology "standing water" wouldn't sitting or lying water be a better definition of what it is actually doing? We meet with the standing buyer (yep, we finally get to meet with the buyer) to discuss the drainage questions, sketch out some solutions, and come to an agreement. The repairs are completed in quick order.

Radon Rhymes With Nothing Funny . . . If Your House Tests Above The Actionable Limit

Ah, but wait, there is a final wrinkle (different final wrinkle). A couple of days later a text scheduling an inspection is received. We wonder what it is all about and make a few calls. It happens that it is not an inspection, but a pickup of the radon testing from the basement. A day or so later the results arrive and it is beyond the "actionable limit".

I inform my wife that the radon readings were above the "actionable limit". We hurriedly grab a few essentials and slowly back out of our house trying not to bump anything and creating a spark, possibly ending life as we know it. We end up at the local diner; Arnold's. Everyone was snickering at the two people walking backwards holding a few essentials, until the Fonz arrived and explained the realities of radon and its effect on leather jackets. 1. Radon is not explosive. 2. You cannot see or smell radon. 3. Radon has no effect on leather jackets. 4. The Fonz did not do a public service announcement for radon, and 5. You might know the Fonz if you are above 40. AAAAAAAAAAAAAAAAAAA!

Anyway, we discuss alternatives with the buyer . . . who I must say by the way, is reasonable and level headed, and doesn't believe that everything we do is to "try and get away with something". I was not accustomed to this kind of buyer and was understandably nervous. After checking for hidden cameras and asking my wife to pinch me a couple times (which she enjoyed way too much), I decided to proceed, albeit with caution. The buyer agrees to allow me to complete the work and also provides me with a contact who does radon remediation for a living. I never met anyone who performs radon remediation for a living — you can imagine what was going through my head. We decided to meet in a public parking lot outside of the local police station .. not really, I call him on the phone . . . he lives in Idaho .. apparently there is radon there also. He provides me with great information and also sizes the anti–radon fan for the house. After much research I have a plan for the installation, order the material, and complete the work. The cost to do it myself is about a third of the estimate I was provided.

I don't like to wait around for the results of my work, I want to know that the completed work is doing what it is supposed to be doing. After sealing the sump and turning the system on, I smoke test around the sump cover. Find a few small leaks, seal them with poly–foam backer rod and the system is nice and tight. I order an electronic radon detection monitor to check the radon levels so I can verify the remediation work is operating correctly. The monitor maintains a seven–day average. A reading above 4.0 is considered "actionable". The first initial reading is 1.6. Yessss, I am a bit more than relieved — slept like a baby that night (once I got my wife to stop pinching me).

Am I recommending you do it yourself? No, I am not. It is hard work. If you don't want a four inch diameter PVC pipe running up the side of your house, it will need to be run inside, from the basement through the roof. There may not be an easy solution. Who wants to be looking at the radon remediation pipe running up the corner of the living room? Then again, it's probably better than the sewer pipe from the upstairs bath running through the corner of the living room. Fortunately, we didn't have that problem. We wanted it to be maintainable, look nice and not have the four inch pipe running up the side of the house. I was able to make it happen without too much remodel work. It required tools that a friend who owns a plumbing company allowed me to use. It requires knowledge of general construction, plumbing, electrical and roofing skills. There are also considerations if you have a gas furnace, gas water heater or gas appliances. Gas appliances do not exist in our home, not sure what happened to them . . . how the heck does our water get hot and our house stay warm in the winter? Oh yeah, electricity! Never mind.

Tip: Radon may be a factor if your home sits on a crawlspace or basement. Do your homework (the internet is a wonderful thing), ask questions about the installation, and get three estimates.

Question #1. If radon is a problem, how do you plan to seal the sump pump?

Question #2. Once the sump is sealed, will it be easy to maintain the sump pump and reassemble the system?

Question #3. How much will it cost?

Question #4. If the remediation method doesn't work, what will be done to fix the problem and will it cost me more money?

Note: send me a check for $19.95 and I will send you an "I love sump–pumps way too much" t–shirt, signed by the author. Or, "I love mud–jacking" – your choice.

The closing that seemed would never arrive, arrives. We meet and sign a multitude of papers and possession of the home is no longer ours. A sad moment that is covered up in the overwhelming amount of work to be done moving a household. The frustration of the showings and the uncertainty of the previous buyers and their inspectors are lost to the ages .. maybe that's a bit too dramatic, but they are quickly becoming a distant memory. A friend asks if I am sad about selling the home . . . at this time, I am not . . . I am happy to be done with it. It has been on my mind and in my dreams each and every day. Wondering what will the buyer want next, what will the inspector find next . . . day in and day out it wears on you. A burden has been lifted from my shoulders. Now I can worry about other burdens that were overshadowed for the moment. There doesn't seem to be a shortage of burdens.

Coordination And Timing – Acquiring The New Domicile

One last thought about moving to your new home. If you are moving to an apartment it shouldn't be a big problem to coordinate the move. Unless the neighborhood is a super cool location. But, for cool people it shouldn't be too hard to find a place and to schedule the move and get your belongings into the apartment.

If you have a bunch of cash laying around and can purchase the new house outright, coordination with the new accommodations shouldn't be a problem either. You can just bring in a suitcase of Benjamin's, buy the place and set up the moving date for your solid gold fixtures and luxury goods.

If you are like me and need to sell your current house for the down payment on your new place the coordination might get a bit tricky. How do I know? Well I can only assume if you have read the previous chapters then you will now understand that nothing goes quite as planned or as hoped. Not saying it can't go that way, but that it didn't go that way in our case. Let me use our case as an example for your reading enjoyment.

With Buyer #1 we were to close May 29th. This was also the closing date set for our new home in Florida. It was almost too good to be true . . . then BAM . . . it wasn't true. Buyer #1 backed out, which could create a slight problem of two mortgages. Then BAM . . . the Florida house goes into probate. I don't want to describe what probate is because I don't really know and if you are that interested feel free to research it and let me know, but suffice to say it's a minimum 90 days. Now what can happen???

This could happen . . . Someone could buy our home and we wouldn't have a place to live while the Florida home is in probate . . . that could happen. Along comes Buyer #2 . . . then they back out . . . we still have a place to live. Then buyer #3 . . . we close, but are close to the end of probate. Will this be a problem?

Maybe. It depends how much flexibility you have regarding your job. My job does allow me to do work and travel for a week or two at a time. We spend the remainder of the first week staying with good friends while we take care of details after the closing and then make our way to Florida where our new home awaits, but is not quite ready. I plan some work travel so I have a place to live (i.e., a hotel) . . . what about my wife . . She can travel with me if needed. She stays with our daughter for the week and tries to not be too much of a bother to her roommate. While I travel for work, the wife and daughter spend a few days at Disney . . . I only write this so that you can see what a dedicated employee and great husband I am . . . I'm not complaining.

I return from the work travel for the weekend and we need a place to stay. We don't want to intrude on our daughter's roommate with another person in the house so we decide to spend the weekend at a Disney Resort. We are Disney Vacation Club Members and have some "points" available. Not only was it a good purchase in the day, but very useful during this transition. It is nice hanging out at a Disney's Saratoga Springs Resort while waiting for your house to close. It can't last forever . . . living at a Disney Resort . . . and it doesn't. It is busy season and there are no more rooms available for the next week so we look for another option.

Fortunately with my work travel I have earned enough Hilton Honors points to book a week at the Hilton Garden Inn next to Sea World. Another nice place to hang out. The hotel has a great breakfast buffet that is better than most restaurants and for Gold and Diamond Hilton Honors members you get a two person voucher . . . excellent.

You may be thinking, why not keep traveling this week? The furniture is delivered this week and there isn't any place to put it. We haven't closed on the house and if it goes into a storage unit the moving company is no longer responsible for the damage. We get permission to store it into the house we do not own . . . could this be a problem? I am sure it can be, but sometimes you have to have a little trust. Did I not learn to trust during the selling phase of the Indiana home . . . not really. We can't insure the contents because we don't own the home. Trust, Hope and Prayer. Also need to get set up in my new office digs so I have a place to do other work when I'm not gallivanting around doing inspections . . . that is once we have a place to call home.

Now, running seriously low of Hilton Honors points it's time to move along, pack up and start inspections again. The wife is along for the ride this trip. Unfortunately it's a different hotel each day and some days are longer than others so she gets to know the staff while she waits in the lobby at the hotel. Another week of hotels and dining out. Contrary to popular belief it does start to get old. I mean really, how much steak and lobster can one person eat?

After a week on the road, we continue to head north and spend the weekend outside of Nashville in Franklin, Tennessee. We have family here, but they are very busy so we only get a short visit with them. Fortunately we are in Franklin. Franklin is a nice place to slow down, take a break, relax, and stroll along the downtown shops doing a little window shopping and when you tire from your shopping, it isn't far to an excellent restaurant, where the food is fine and the staff friendly. While window shopping we did run across a pillow with the saying . . . "There's no place like home" It's funny but true. It is nice to have a place to hang your hat.

We have another three concrete plant inspections this week (that's three more nights we have a place to live), but this time the plants are within driving distance from a single hotel. My wife no longer has to wait in the lobby for me to pick her up each day, she can hang out. She especially likes this hotel and gets to know the staff. Apparently celebrities are staying at our hotel and one is particularly famous, and while I know the show I wouldn't recognize him because the last show I saw him in was Malcolm in the Middle.

While interesting to stalk celebrities, I still have to inspect concrete plants and get up early. No time for celebrities, this is the real world, we have to keep moving. With the plant inspections complete we are off to Kentucky to pick up our son for a family friend's wedding. We spend the night and drive to Illinois for the family wedding. After two nights in Illinois it's back to Kentucky to drop the son off at school. We continue driving and spend another hotel night somewhere along the way. Anywhere as long as it is past Atlanta, because traffic in Atlanta is not fun. You need a week's vacation from the stress of driving through that city. We get back into Florida and the house is still not ready to close. We spend another night with our daughter.

Word is the closing will take place the coming Friday. This time it sounds like the real deal. We actually begin to make arrangements. First, we make arrangements using our DVC points (this is the last of them) for the week at Disney's Saratoga Springs Resort. I find it is very hard to get up and leave for work from a Disney Resort. Things are progressing swimmingly. Thursday I call my bank to ask what information they will need from me to make the wire transfer. I am told that they cannot make a wire transfer unless I am physically at the bank. This is not good news, because the closest bank branch is in Kentucky and I am in Florida. There is no way around it, my wife and I leave Orlando a night early from the Disney Resort, losing our points, and at 6 pm, after a full day of work, we head north.

We drive until 3am until we are past Atlanta, get up and are back on the road at 7am. We arrive at the bank branch just a hop, skip and a jump from Florida, just a bit south of Cincinnati at 3pm. The wire transfer to the title company proceeds with no problem and we hop in the car and go celebrate with a bowl of Gold Star Chili (doesn't everyone). Our son is graced with another night's visit from his parents. We plan to leave Saturday, but I am beginning to feel the effects of this quick trip. We spend another night and leave Sunday morning for Florida.

We drive nonstop to Orlando and spend the night with our daughter. Up early we visit with our Florida Realtor and tour the house, then we are off to the closing. There is a slight two hour delay, but the mountains of paperwork are eventually signed. After only six weeks of living in hotels or spending a few nights with our children we are officially Florida Homeowners. That wasn't so bad.

What If I Could Do It Again?

• Next time, I will not move.

• Rent.

• Start years before I know I want to move aka don't procrastinate home projects.

• Win the lottery and buy all new house, furniture, cars, and clothing. This option sounds nice.

Of course I kid I kid . . . Next time I will do as described above concerning repairs and improvements. The repairs will be done quickly, there will be no delay, and no time will be wasted. I will not wait until we decide to move. Unless of course we don't have the money or just don't feel like it. Lack of funds could also cause a small delay. You may have experienced this feeling before... but sometimes we have to save, the credit card limit will only go so high . . . and that is probably higher than it should be allowed.

I believe we prepared for the move in the appropriate manner and using the winter months to our advantage to clean up, touch up and pack up. The home was listed in the middle of March, prior to Spring Break and about the time people are looking forward to getting out of the house and finding a new place to live. As you now know the sale moved forward rather quickly, there were good offers, but buyers are a fickle lot and you never know what they might request.

Final Thoughts In 176 Words . . . Now That Is Concise

It is a matter of patience and knowing that not every buyer is the buyer, but also know that your buyer is out there looking for the qualities that your home offers. It may take time for them to find you, fall in love with your house. and then run you through the grinder . . . oh wait that is the person who is not the one.

Don't be in a hurry, don't give the appearance that you need to sell and don't get angry with buyer requests and inspection reports. Look at your home honestly, prior to listing, and find a realtor that specializes in your neighborhood and has the experience and expertise to provide you with the guidance to navigate the home selling process.

This story is just our experience. Your experience will hopefully be smoother and maybe the pearls of wisdom within these pages have given you the insight that can assist you in the pursuit of the elusive buyer. Because c'mon, selling a house is fun!

Best of luck to you selling your home.

Acknowledgements

Cindy Martin, Thank you for your great advice and helpful insights along the way as Wendy and I journeyed with you to sell the home. The ups and downs along the way were not at all frightening as you provided us with your wisdom, professional understanding, and good humor as we proceeded down the home seller's rabbit hole.

Chet Skwarcan, for so many reviews and edits I have lost count. From start to finish it was always fun to create because of your encouragement and effort

Chet Skwarcan, award–winning engineer, writer and industry innovator in the field of traffic engineering is one of the most sought after thought leaders in leveraging creativity, logic and technology to solve today's engineering challenges. An originator of applying crowd–sourced collaboration techniques to online traffic data, his strategy and data has been adopted by international technology brands including Google. Residing in central Indiana, Chet spends his free time flying drones, and spending quality time with his wife and their four amazing children. To learn more about Chet, visit *www.TrafficEngineering.com*

About the Author

Doug Wilcoxon was raised in Cantrall, Illinois, Population 100. It was a great place to grow up. The street where he lived with his mom, dad and two brothers has not yet been set aside as a national park.

Doug Is A:

Husband and Father of two (children).

Graduate of Lincoln Land Community College and the University of Illinois at Urbana–Champaign.

Professional Engineer in Indiana and Florida.

Writer of stories

Walt Disney World Fan

Home Repairman and DIYer.

Lover of Coney Dogs with his own special recipe

Fan of Aunt Dodi's Blue Ribbon Peanut Brittle and English Toffee

www.ingramcontent.com/pod-product-compliance
Lightning Source LLC
Chambersburg PA
CBHW051223170526
45166CB00005B/2014